HAL LEONARD
STUDENT
PIANO
LIBRARY

Late Elementary–Intermediate Level

Christmas Anthology

30 Holiday Arrangements for Piano Solo
For All Piano Methods

CONTENTS

ISBN 978-1-4950-6984-0

HAL•LEONARD®
CORPORATION
7777 W. BLUEMOUND RD. P.O. BOX 13819 MILWAUKEE, WI 53213

Visit Hal Leonard Online at
www.halleonard.com

Late Elementary

Blue Christmas

Words and Music by Billy Hayes
and Jay Johnson
Arranged by Phillip Keveren

Moderately (♩ = 112)

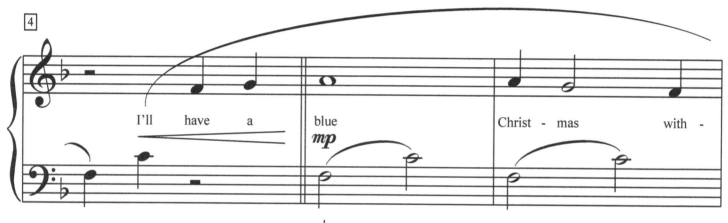

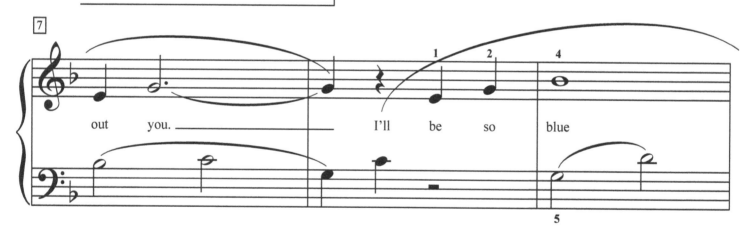

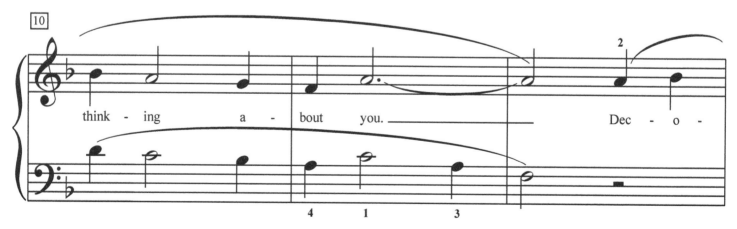

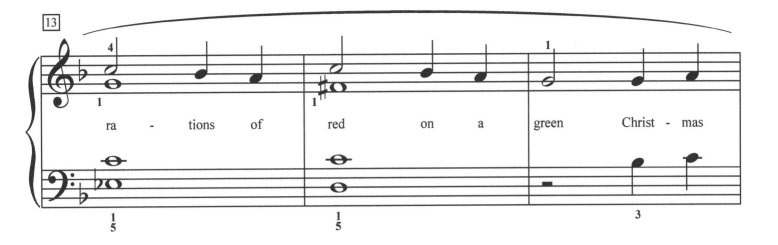

ra - tions of red on a green Christ - mas

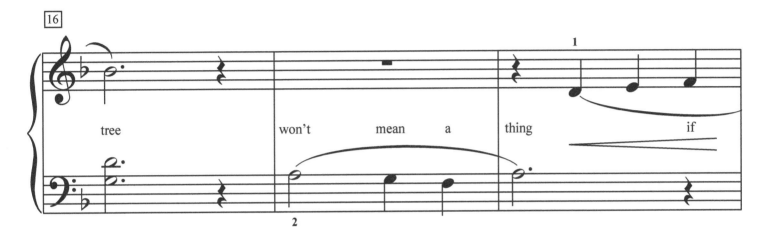

tree won't mean a thing if

you're not here with me. I'll have a blue

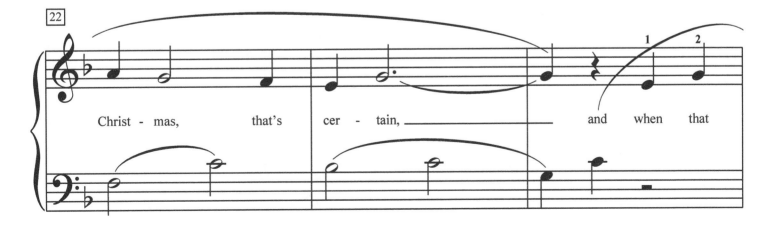

Christ - mas, that's cer - tain, and when that

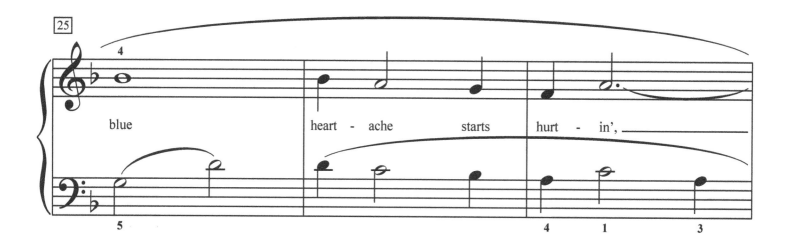

blue _____ heart - ache starts hurt - in', _____

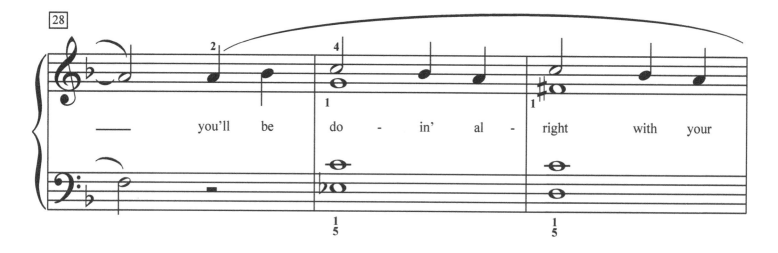

_____ you'll be do - in' al - right with your

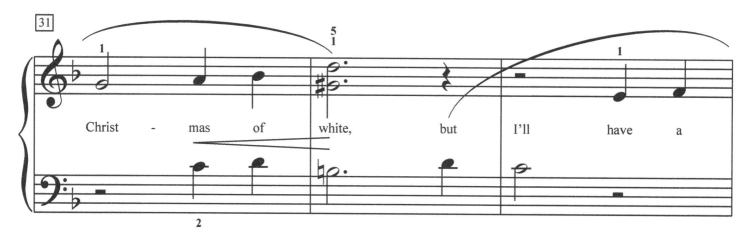

Christ - mas of white, but I'll have a

blue, blue Christ - mas.

Frosty the Snow Man

Words and Music by Steve Nelson
and Jack Rollins

Frost - y the Snow Man was a jol - ly hap - py soul, with a
Frost - y the Snow Man knew the sun was hot that day, so he

corn cob pipe and a but - ton nose and two eyes made out of coal.
said, "Let's run and we'll have some fun now be - fore I melt a - way."

Frost - y the Snow Man is a fair - y tale they say; he was
Down to the vil - lage with a broom-stick in his hand, he run-ning

made of snow but the chil - dren know how he came to life one day. There
here and there all a - round the square say-ing, "Catch me if you can." He

must have been some mag - ic in that old silk hat they found, for
led them down the streets of town right to the traf - fic cop, and he

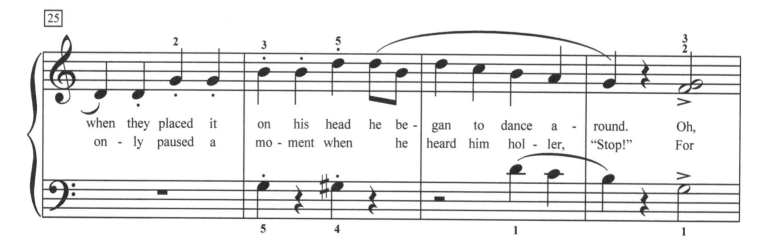

when they placed it on his head he be - gan to dance a - round. Oh,
on - ly paused a mo - ment when he heard him hol - ler, "Stop!" For

8

Frost - y the Snow Man was a - live as he could be, and the
Frost - y the Snow Man had to hur - ry on his way, but he

chil - dren say he could laugh and play just the same as you and me.
waved good - bye say - in' "Don't you cry; I'll be back a - gain some - day."

Thump-et - y thump thump, thump-et - y thump thump, look at Frost - y go!

mp

Thump-et - y thump thump, thump-et - y thump thump, o - ver the hills of snow.

mf

f

9

Rockin' Around the Christmas Tree

Music and Lyrics by
Johnny Marks

With a bounce (Swing eighths)

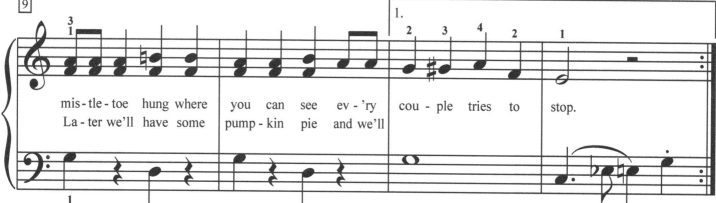

Rock-in' a - round the Christ-mas tree at the Christ-mas par - ty hop;
Rock-in' a - round the Christ-mas tree; let the Christ-mas spir - it ring.

mis-tle-toe hung where you can see ev-'ry cou-ple tries to stop.
La-ter we'll have some pump-kin pie and we'll

do some car-ol-ing. You will get a sen-ti-ment-al feel-ing when you

Rudolph the Red-Nosed Reindeer

Music and Lyrics by
Johnny Marks

9 Moderately, with a lilt

Ru - dolph the Red - Nosed Rein - deer had a ver - y shin - y
All of the oth - er rein - deer used to laugh and call him

mf

12

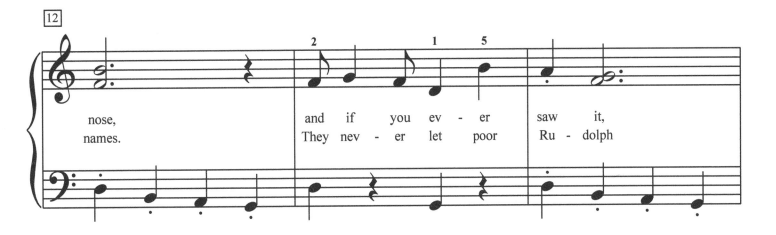

nose, and if you ev - er saw it,
names. They nev - er let poor Ru - dolph

15

1.
you would e - ven say it glows.

2.
join in an - y rein - deer

18

games. Then one fog - gy Christ - mas Eve, San - ta came to

p

13

say, "Ru - dolph with your nose so bright, won't you guide my

sleigh to - night? __ Then all the rein - deer loved him,

as they shout-ed out with glee: "Ru-dolph the Red-Nosed Rein - deer,

you'll go down in his - to - ry!"

Silver and Gold

Music and Lyrics by
Johnny Marks
Arranged by Carol Klose

15

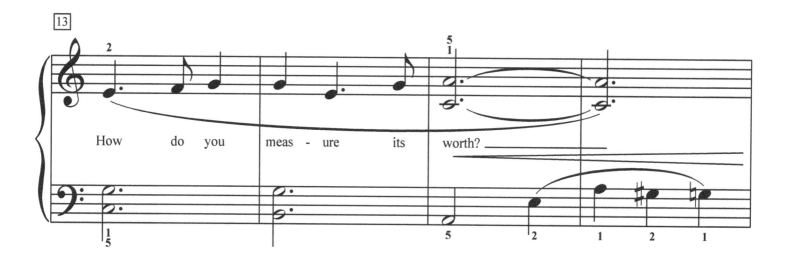

How do you meas - ure its worth? ___

Just by the pleas - ure it gives here on

earth? Sil - ver and gold,

mp

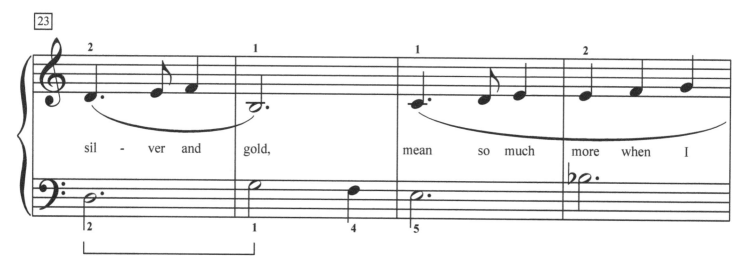

sil - ver and gold, mean so much more when I

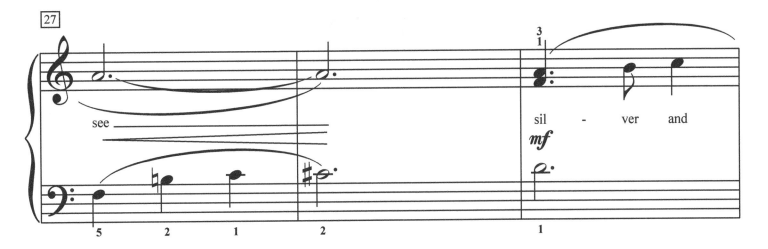

see _____ sil - ver and

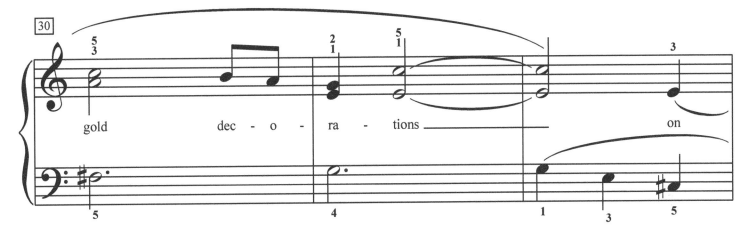

gold dec - o - ra - tions _____ on

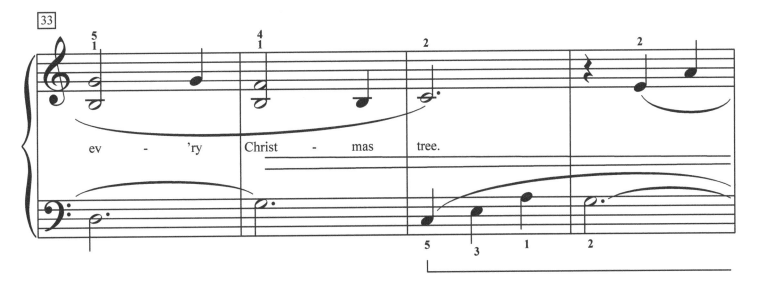

ev - 'ry Christ - mas tree.

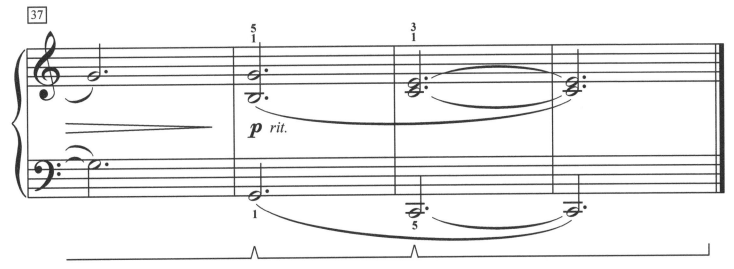

p *rit.*

Suzy Snowflake

Words and Music by Sid Tepper
and Roy Bennett
Arranged by Fred Kern

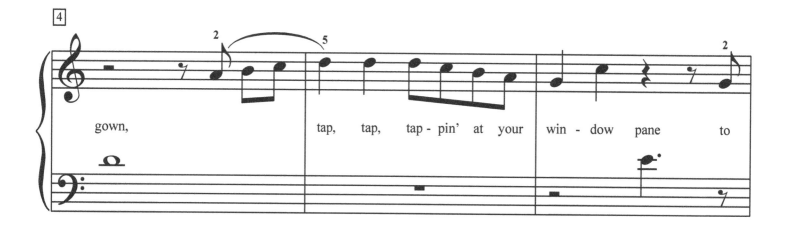

Accompaniment (Student plays one octave higher than written.)

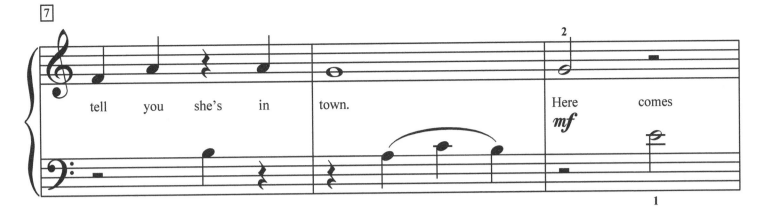

tell you she's in town. Here comes *mf*

Su - zy Snow - flake, soon you will hear her say:

"Come out ev - 'ry - one and play with me; I have - n't long to

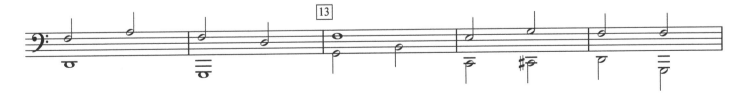

Here   comes   Su - zy   Snow - flake,   look   at   her   tum - blin'

mf

down,   Bring - ing   joy   to   ev - 'ry   girl   and   boy;

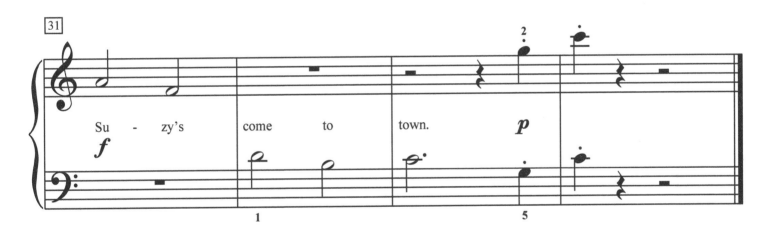

Su - zy's   come   to   town.   *p*

f

Early Intermediate

Believe
from Warner Bros. Pictures' THE POLAR EXPRESS

Words and Music by Glen Ballard
and Alan Silvestri
Arranged by Fred Kern

dream - ers ____ not so long ____ a - go, ____
sail - ing ____ far a - cross ____ the sea, ____

but one by one, we ____ all had to grow ____ up.
trust - ing star - light ____ to get where they need to be.

When it seems the mag - ic slipped a - way, we find it all a - gain on Christ-mas
When it seems that we have lost our way, we find our-selves a - gain on Christ-mas

mf

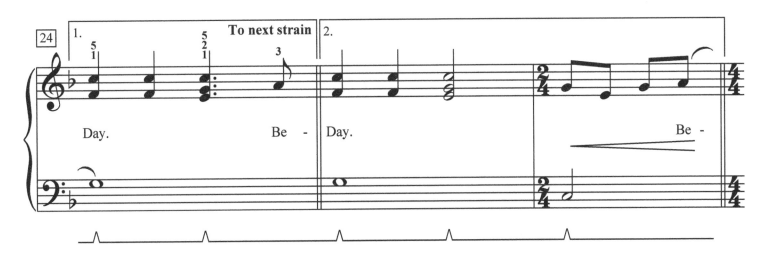

1.
To next strain 2.

Day. Be - Day. Be -

lieve in what your heart is say-ing, hear the mel - o - dy that's play-ing. There's no time to waste, there's so

much to cel - e - brate. Be - lieve in what you feel in - side and give your dreams the wings to

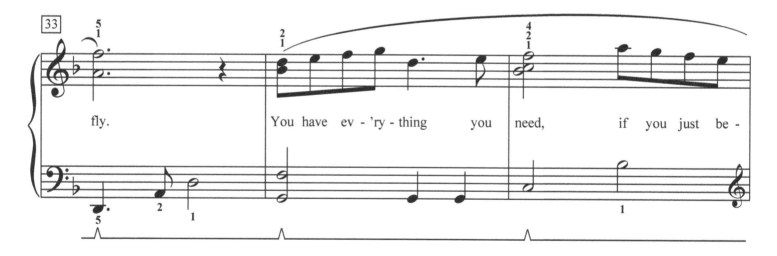

fly. You have ev - 'ry - thing you need, if you just be -

1.
lieve.

2.
lieve.

If you just be -

lieve,

mf if you just be - lieve,

if you just be - lieve. *p*

Just be -

lieve,

mp just be - lieve.

Repeat and Fade

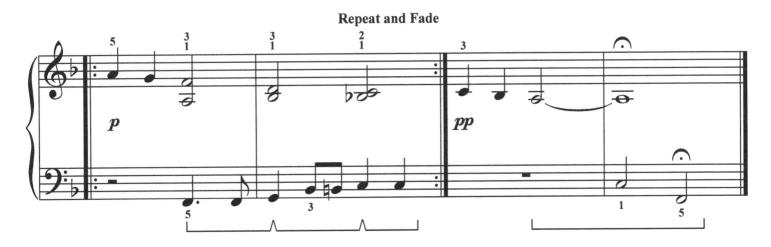

p

pp

27

Feliz Navidad

Music and Lyrics by
José Feliciano

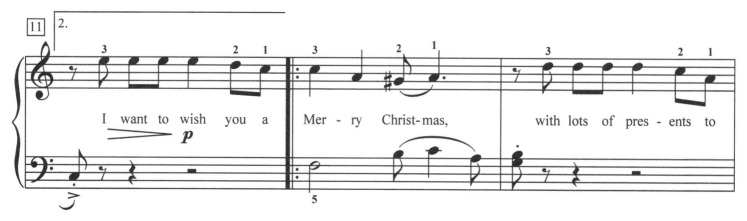

make you hap-py. I want to wish you a Mer - ry Christ-mas from the

bot-tom of my heart. _____ I want to wish you a Fe - liz Na-vi-

dad. Fe - liz Na-vi - dad. Fe - liz Na-vi-

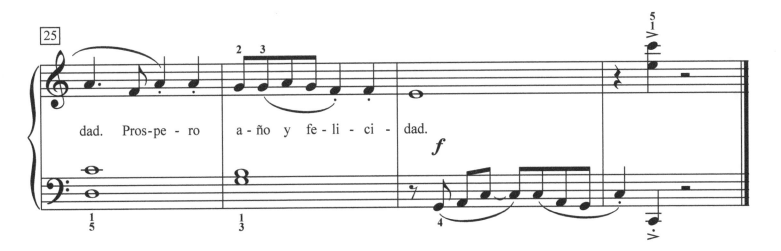

dad. Pros-pe - ro a - ño y fe-li - ci - dad.

Grandma Got Run Over by a Reindeer

Words and Music by
Randy Brooks
Arranged by Jennifer Linn

as for me and Grand - pa, we be - lieve.

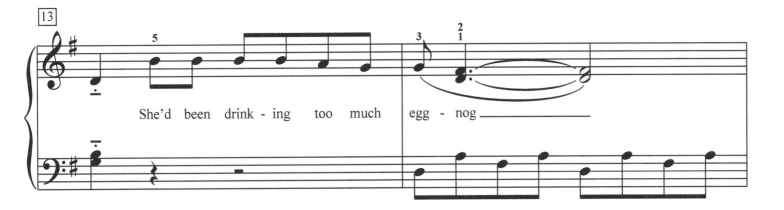

She'd been drink - ing too much egg - nog _____

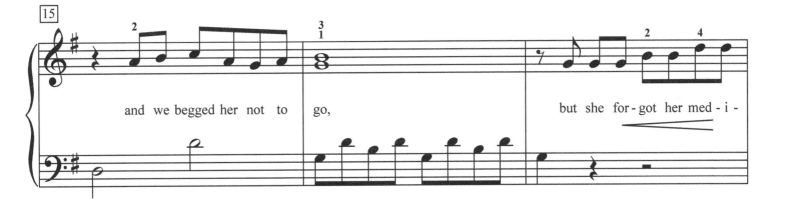

and we begged her not to go, but she for - got her med - i -

ca - tion, _____ and she stag-gered out the door in - to the snow.

When we found her Christ-mas morn-ing ____

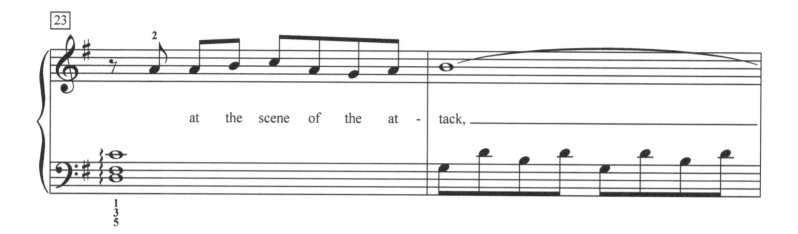

at the scene of the at-tack, ____

____ she had hoof-prints on her fore-head, ____ and in-

crim-i-nat-ing Claus marks on her back. Grand-ma got run o-ver by a

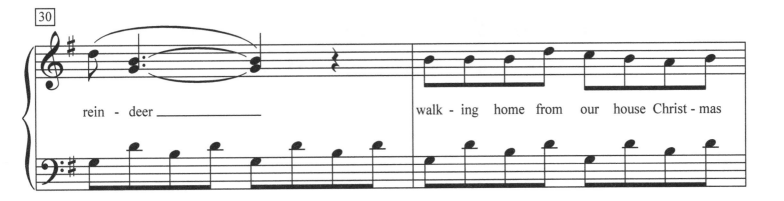

rein - deer _____ walk - ing home from our house Christ - mas

Eve. You can say there's no such thing as

San - ta, _____ but as for me and Grand - pa, we be -

lieve. _____

It's Beginning to Look Like Christmas

*12/8 is like two measures of 6/8.

By Meredith Willson

It's be - gin-ning to look a lot like
gin-ning to look a lot like

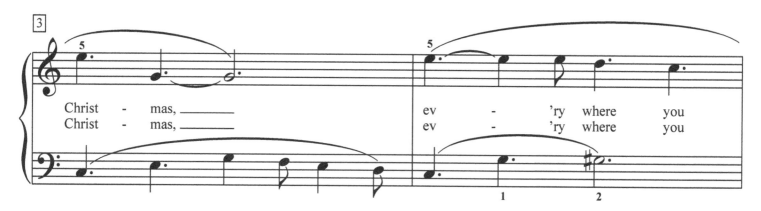

Christ - mas,＿＿＿ ev - 'ry where you
Christ - mas,＿＿＿ ev - 'ry where you

go; take a look in the five and ten,
go; there's a tree in the grand ho - tel,

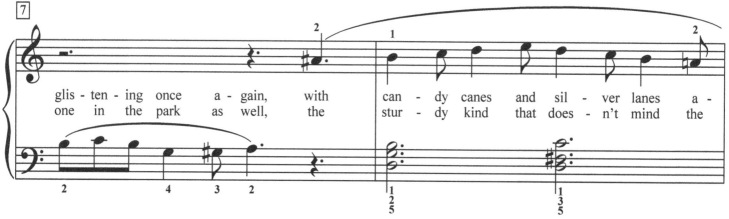

glis - ten - ing once a - gain, with
one in the park as well, with the
can - dy canes and sil - ver lanes a -
stur - dy kind that does - n't mind the

glow.   It's be - gin - ning to look a lot like
snow.   It's be - gin - ning to look a lot like

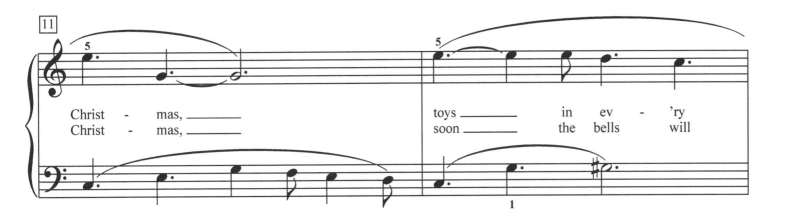

Christ - mas, _____   toys _____ in ev - 'ry
Christ - mas, _____   soon _____ the bells will

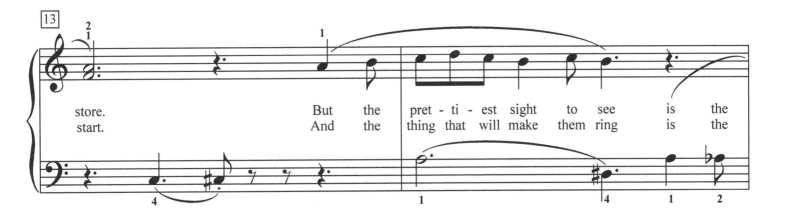

store.   But the pret - ti - est sight to see is the
start.   And the thing that will make them ring is the

To Coda ⊕

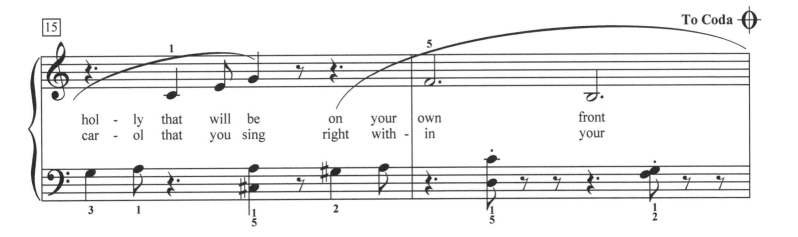

hol - ly that will be on your own   front
car - ol that you sing right with - in   your

35

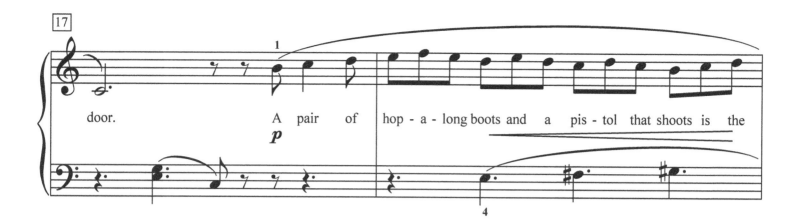

door. A pair of hop-a-long boots and a pis-tol that shoots is the

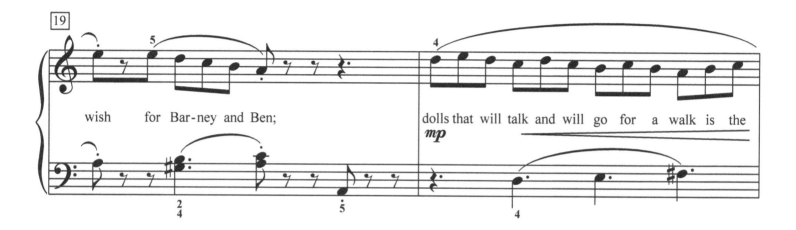

wish for Bar-ney and Ben; dolls that will talk and will go for a walk is the

hope of Jan-ice and Jen. And Mom and Dad can hard-ly wait for

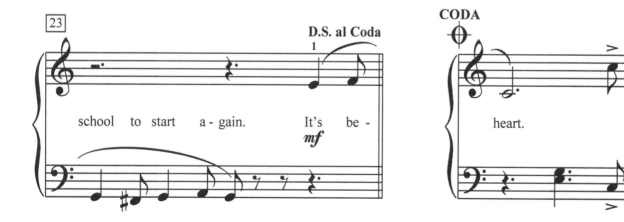

school to start a-gain. It's be- heart.

The Little Drummer Boy

Words and Music by Harry Simeone,
Henry Onorati and Katherine Davis
Arranged by Jennifer and Mike Watts

fore the King, pa | rum pum pum pum, | rum pum pum pum, | rum pum pum pum, ___

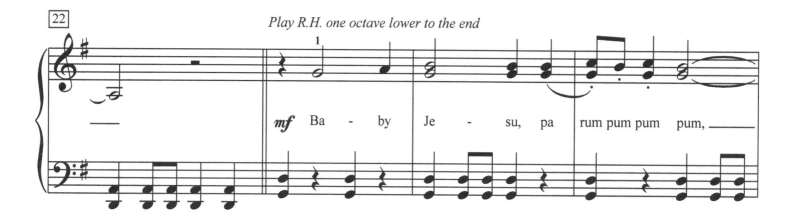

Play R.H. one octave lower to the end

___ | *mf* Ba - by Je - su, pa | rum pum pum pum, ___

___ | I am a poor boy, too, pa | rum pum pum pum. ___

___ | I have no gift to bring, pa | rum pum pum pum, ___

38

that's fit to give our King, pa rum pum pum pum,

rum pum pum pum, rum pum pum pum. Shall I

play for you, pa rum pum pum pum. on my drum? *dim. poco a poco*

p

Jingle Bell Rock

Words and Music by Joe Beal
and Jim Boothe

Jin-gle bell, jin-gle bell, jin-gle bell rock, jin-gle bell swing and jin-gle bells ring.
Jin-gle bell, jin-gle bell, jin-gle bell rock, jin-gle bells chime in jin-gle bell time,

Snow-in' and blow-in' up bush-els of fun, now the jin-gle hop has be-gun.
danc-in' and pranc-in' in Jin-gle Bell Square

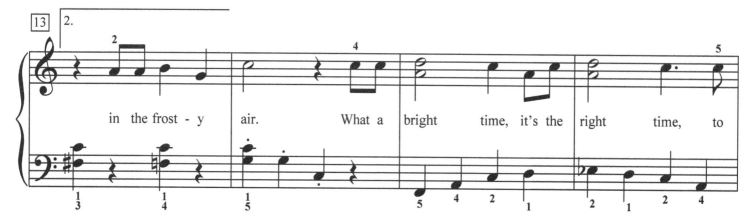

in the frost-y air. What a bright time, it's the right time, to

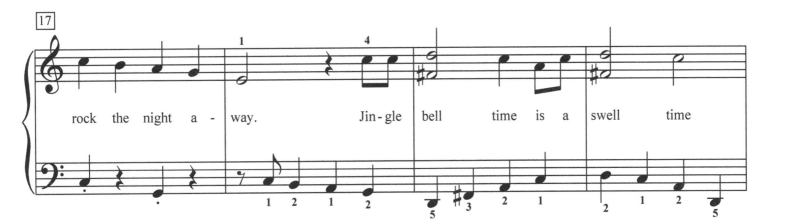

rock the night a - way. Jin - gle bell time is a swell time

to go glid-in' in a one-horse sleigh. Gid-dy - ap, jin-gle horse, pick up your feet,

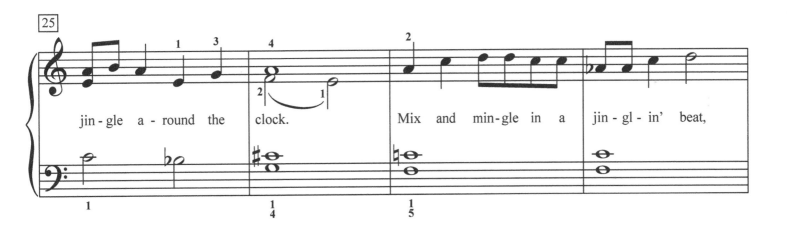

jin - gle a - round the clock. Mix and min-gle in a jin - gl - in' beat,

that's the jin - gle bell, that's the jin - gle bell, that's the jin - gle bell rock.

Silver Bells
from the Paramount Picture THE LEMON DROP KID

Words and Music by Jay Livingston
and Ray Evans

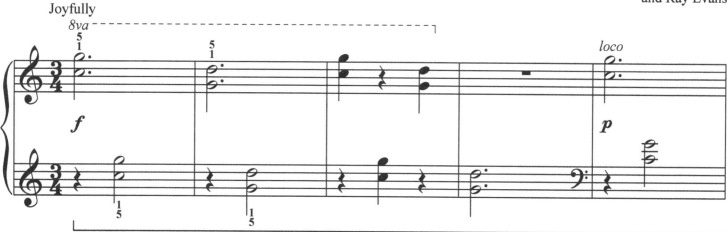

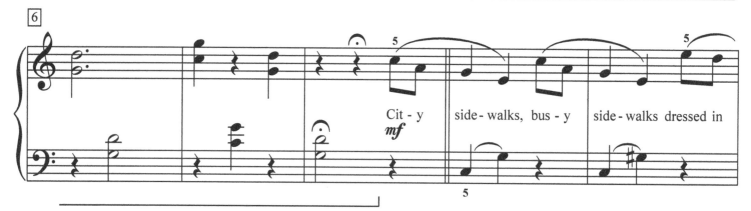

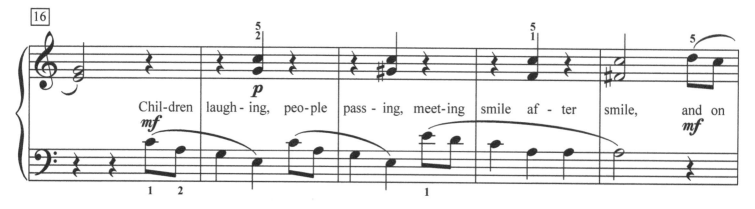

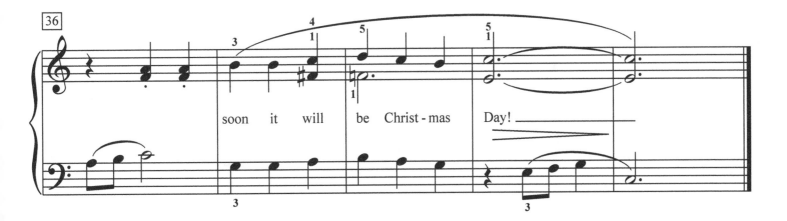

Santa Claus Is Comin' to Town

Words by Haven Gillespie
Music by J. Fred Coots
Arranged by Phillip Keveren

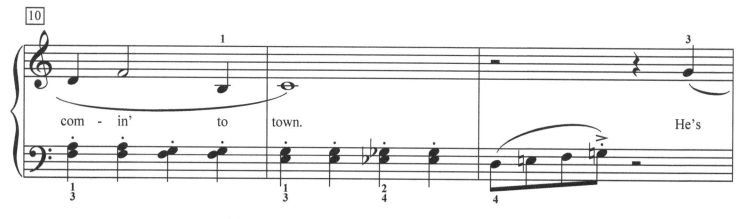

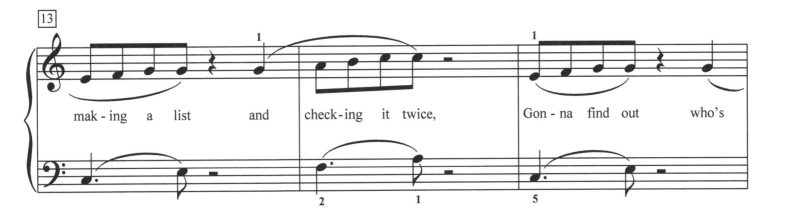

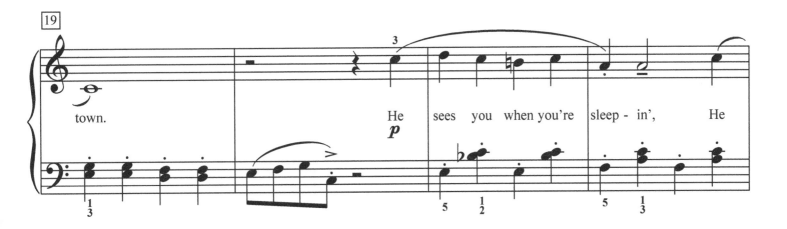

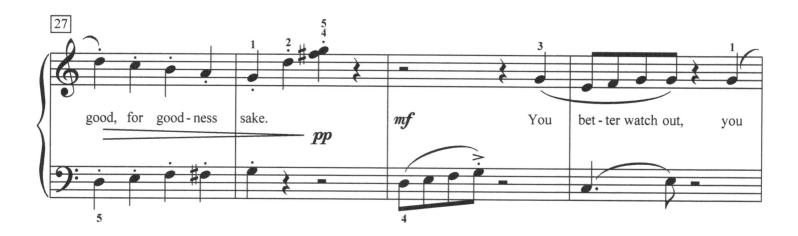

good, for good-ness sake. *pp* *mf* You bet-ter watch out, you

bet-ter not cry, Bet-ter not pout, I'm tell-ing you why:

San-ta Claus is com-in', *p* San-ta Claus is *mp*

com-in', San-ta Claus is com-in' to town! *mf* *f*

Snowfall

Lyrics by Ruth Thornhill
Music by Claude Thornhill
Arranged by Phillip Keveren

Floating dreamily (♩ = 84)

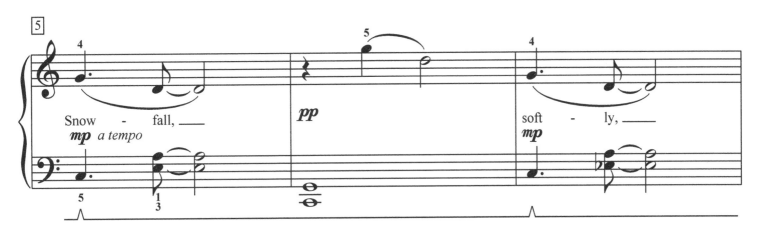

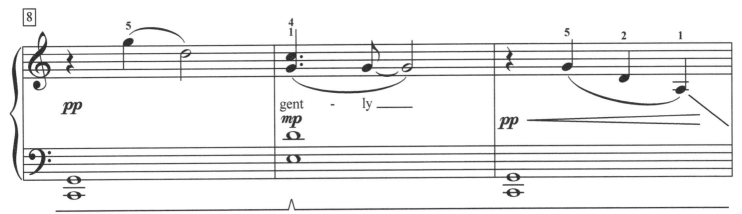

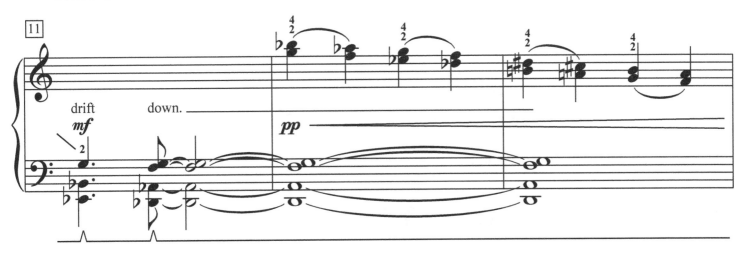

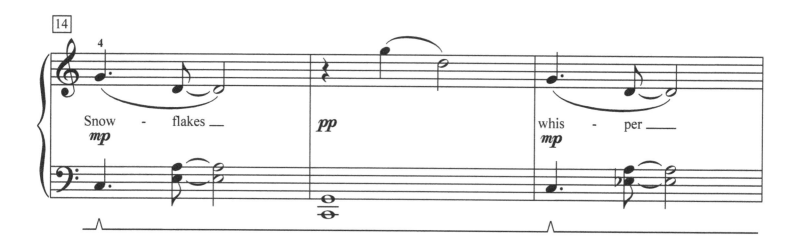

Snow - flakes ___ *pp* whis - per ___
mp *mp*

pp 'neath my ___ *pp*
mp

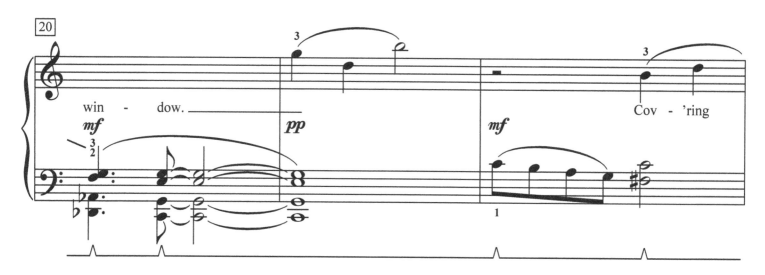

win - dow. ___ *pp* Cov - 'ring
mf *mf*

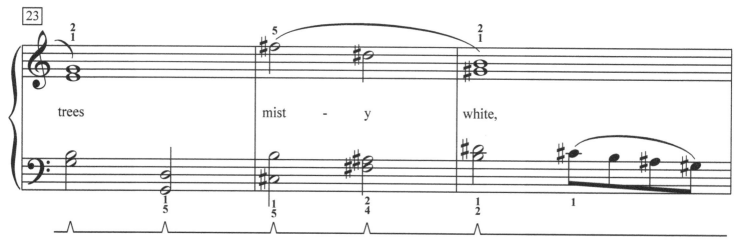

trees mist - y white,

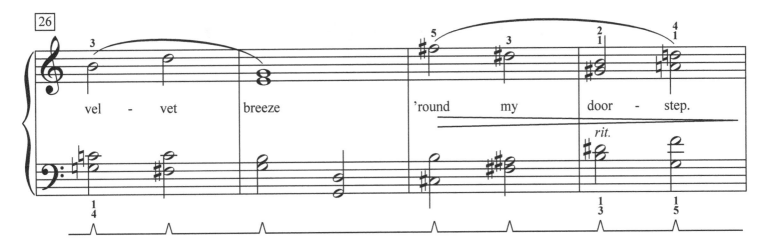

vel - vet breeze 'round my door - step.

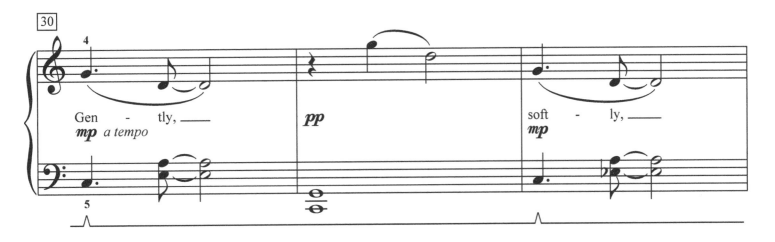

Gen - tly, _____ *pp* soft - ly, _____
mp *a tempo* *mp*

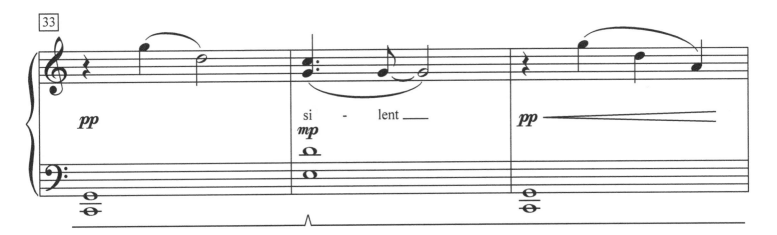

pp si - lent _____ *pp*
mp

snow - fall! _____
mf *rit.* *pp*

Winter Wonderland

Words by Dick Smith
Music by Felix Bernard
Arranged by Jennifer and Mike Watts

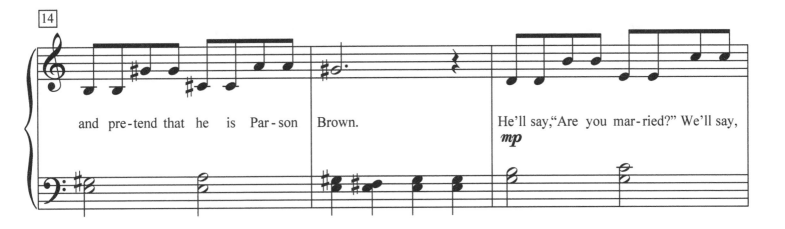

and pre-tend that he is Par-son Brown. He'll say, "Are you mar-ried?" We'll say,

"No, man! But you can do the job when you're in town!" Lat-er on, we'll con-

spire, ___ as we dream by the fire, ___ to face un-a-fraid, the

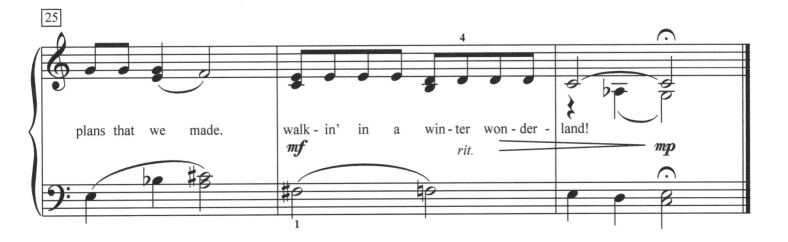

plans that we made. walk-in' in a win-ter won-der-land!

Wonderful Christmastime

Words and Music by
Paul McCartney
Arranged by Mona Rejino

17 Sim - ply hav - ing a won - der - ful Christ - mas - time.

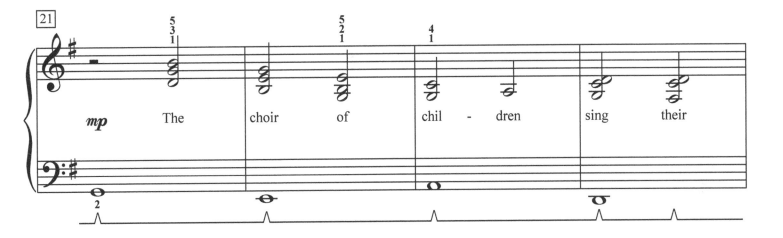

21 *mp* The choir of chil - dren sing their

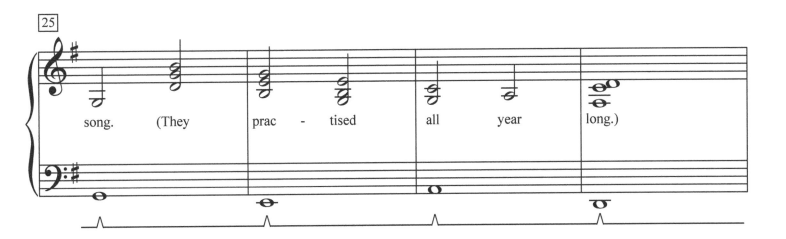

25 song. (They prac - tised all year long.)

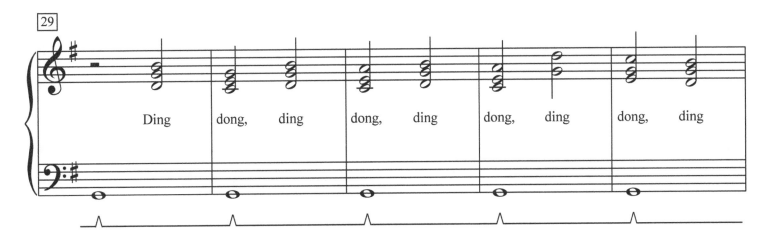

29 Ding dong, ding dong, ding dong, ding dong, ding

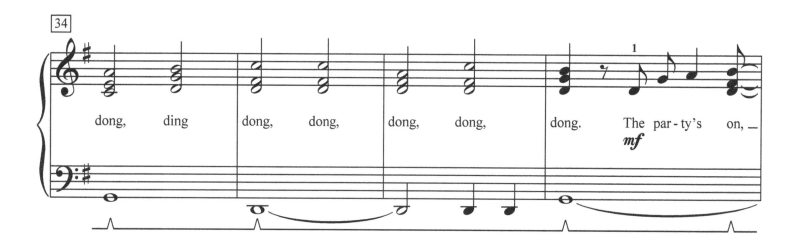

dong, ding dong, dong, dong, dong, dong. The par-ty's on,

the spir-it's up, we're here to-night

and that's e-nough. Sim — ply
sim — ply

hav — ing a won-der-ful Christ-mas — time. We're
hav — ing a won-der-ful Christ-mas — time.

time.

Intermediate

Christmas Time Is Here
from A CHARLIE BROWN CHRISTMAS

Words by Lee Mendelson
Music by Vince Guaraldi
Arranged by Phillip Keveren

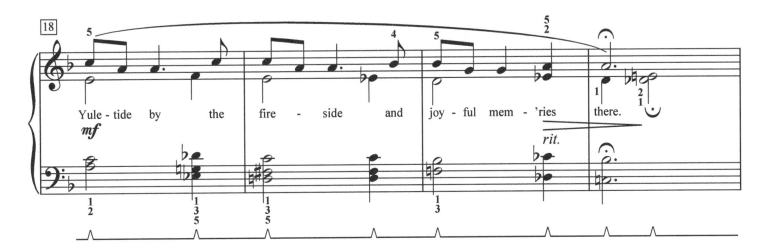

Yule - tide by the fire - side and joy - ful mem - 'ries there.

mf
rit.

mp
a tempo

Christ-mas time is here, we'll be draw - ing near.

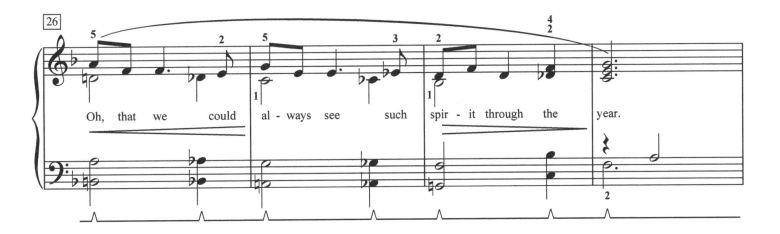

Oh, that we could al - ways see such spir - it through the year.

mf
molto rit.
pp

The Christmas Waltz

Words by Sammy Cahn
Music by Jule Styne

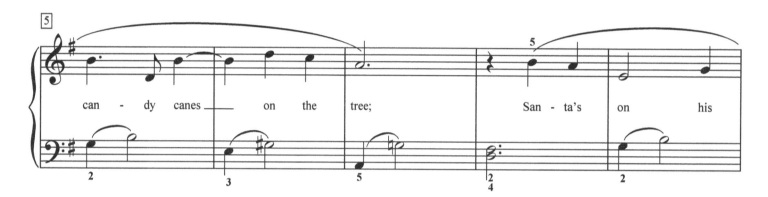

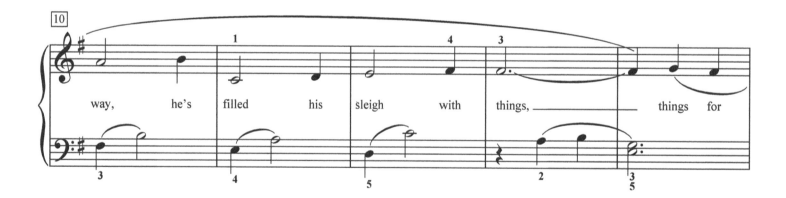

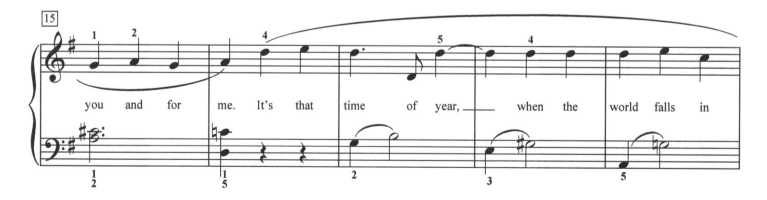

love, Ev - 'ry song you hear ___ seems to say; ___ "Mer - ry

Christ - mas, ___ May your New Year dreams come true." ___

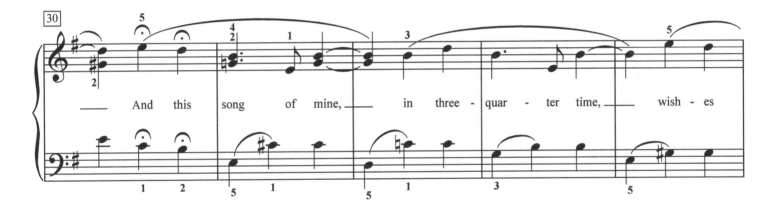

___ And this song of mine, ___ in three - quar - ter time, ___ wish - es

you and yours ___ the same thing too.

Have Yourself a Merry Little Christmas

from MEET ME IN ST. LOUIS

Words and Music by Hugh Martin
and Ralph Blane
Arranged by Jennifer and Mike Watts

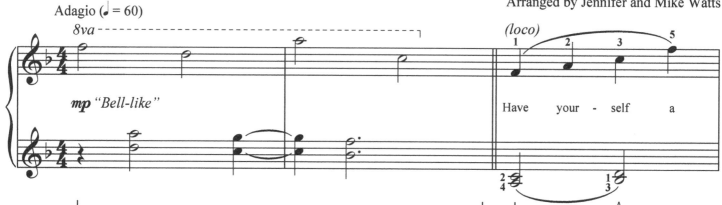

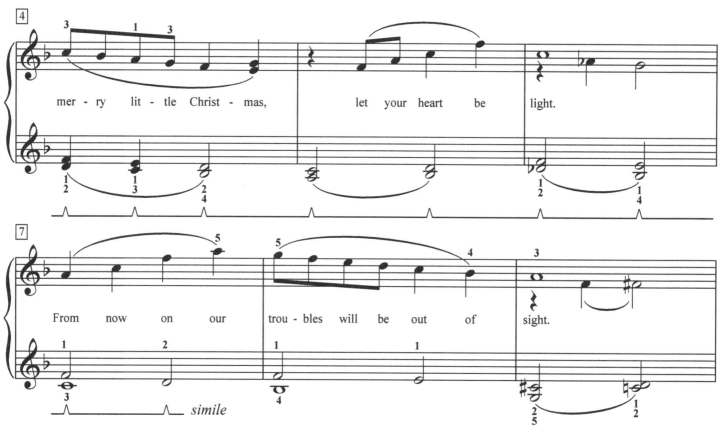

make the Yule - tide gay. From now on our trou-bles will be miles a -

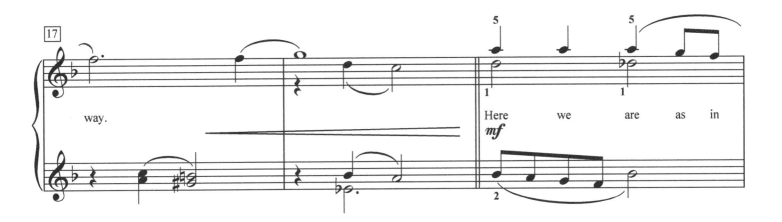

way. Here we are as in

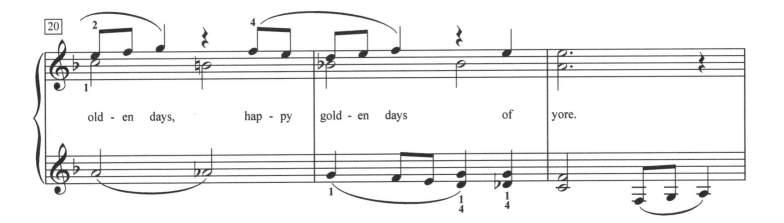

old - en days, hap - py gold - en days of yore.

Faith - ful friends who are dear to us gath - er near to us once

more. Through the years we all will be to-geth-er, if the fates al-

mp

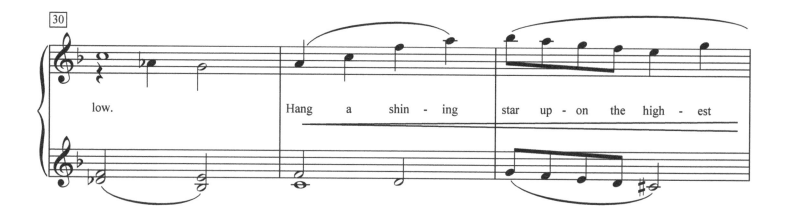

low. Hang a shin-ing star up-on the high-est

bough. and have your-self

f *mp*

a mer-ry lit-tle Christ-mas now.

loco *rit.* *a tempo*

Let It Go
from FROZEN

Music and Lyrics by Kristen Anderson-Lopez
and Robert Lopez
Arranged by Jennifer Linn

Half-time feel, mysterious ($\quad$ = 69)

p

With pedal

The

snow glows white on the moun-tain to-night;__ not a foot-print _____ to be seen. __

A king-dom of i - so - la - tion, and it

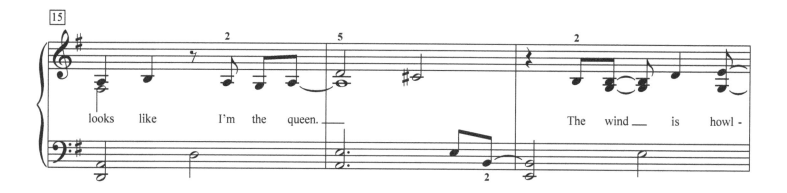

looks like I'm the queen.___ The wind___ is howl-

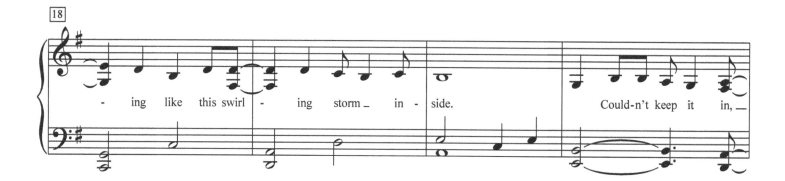

-ing like this swirl - ing storm___ in - side. Could-n't keep it in,___

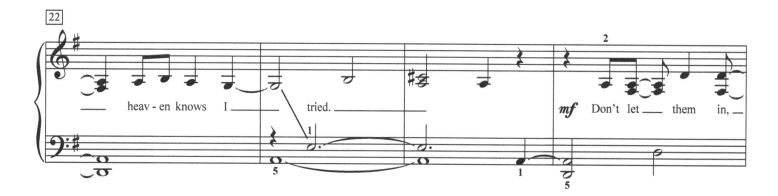

___ heav - en knows I ___ tried.___ *mf* Don't let ___ them in,___

___ don't let ___ them see; ___ be the good girl you al - ways have ___ to

be. Con - ceal,___ don't feel, don't let ___ them know... *cresc.*

Well, now ___ they know. ___ Let it go, ___

(2nd time R.H. 8va)

let it go; ___ can't ___ hold it back an-y-more. I am one with the wind and sky. ___
let it go; ___

Let it go, ___ let it go; ___ turn a-way ___
Let it go, ___ let it go; ___ you'll nev-

___ and slam ___ the ___ door. ___ I don't ___ care ___ Here I ___ stand,
-er see ___ me ___ cry. ___

To Coda ⊕

___ what they're going to ___ say; ___ let the storm rage ___ on. ___
and here I'll ___ stay; ___ let the storm rage ___ on. ___

The cold nev-er both-ered me an-y-way.

It's fun-ny how some

dis-tance makes ev-'ry-thing___ seem small; and the

fears that once___ con-trolled me can't get to me___ at

all. It's time___ to see___ what I___ can do,___

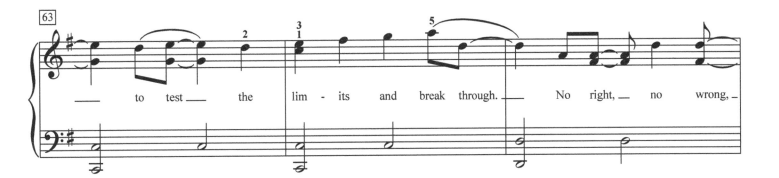

to test the lim - its and break through. No right, no wrong,

no rules for me, I'm free!

cresc.

D.S. al Coda

Let it go,

f

CODA *(loco)*

f

My pow - er flur - ries through the air in - to the

ground.   My soul ___ is   spi - ral - ing   in

fro - zen   frac - tals   all   a - round. ___   And one ___   thought

crys - tal - liz - es   like   an   i - cy   blast:

_f_ I'm nev - er   go - ing back; ___   the   past   is in ___ the past! ___   _cresc._
        _mf_

Let   it   go,   let   it   go, ___   and   I'll   rise ___
_ff_

like the break of dawn. Let it go, let it go;

that per-fect girl is gone. Here I stand

in the light of day;

let the storm rage on.

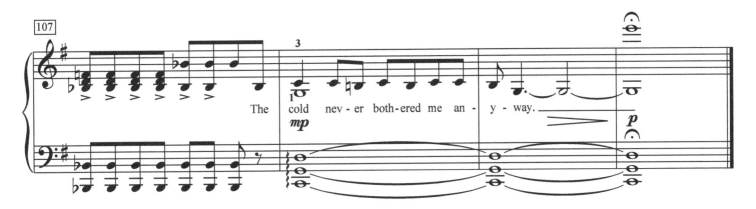

The cold nev-er both-ered me an-y-way.

mp

p

69

Let It Snow! Let It Snow! Let It Snow!

Words by Sammy Cahn
Music by Jule Styne

Moderately, with a lilt

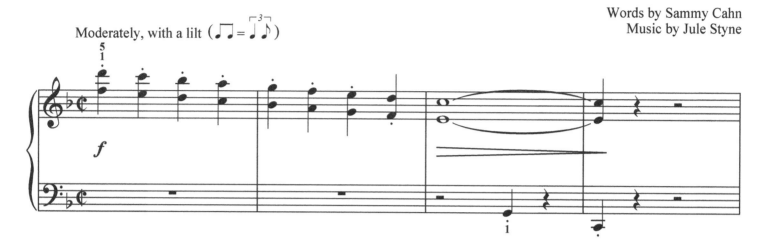

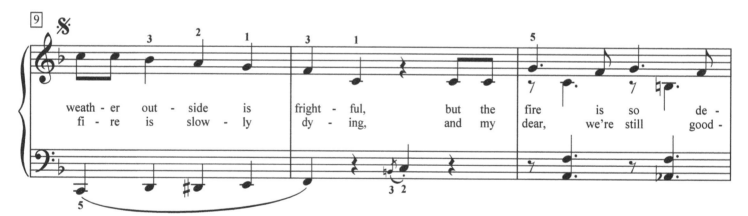

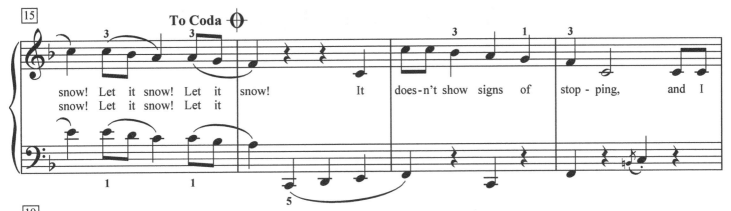

snow! Let it snow! Let it snow! It does-n't show signs of stop - ping, and I
snow! Let it snow! Let it

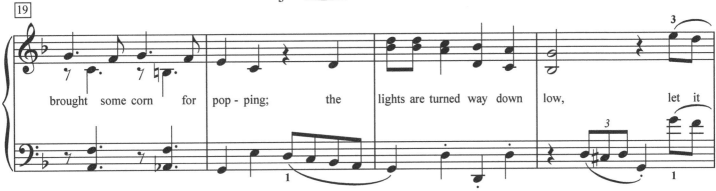

brought some corn for pop - ping; the lights are turned way down low, let it

snow! Let it snow! Let it snow! When we fi - nal - ly kiss good - night, how I'll

hate go - ing out in the storm! But if you'll real - ly hold me tight,

all the way home I'll be warm. The

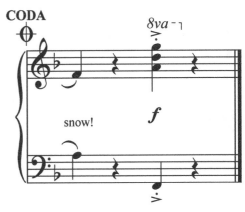

snow!

Linus and Lucy

By Vince Guaraldi
Arranged by Mona Rejino

D.S. al Coda

CODA

Mister Santa

Words and Music by
Pat Ballard

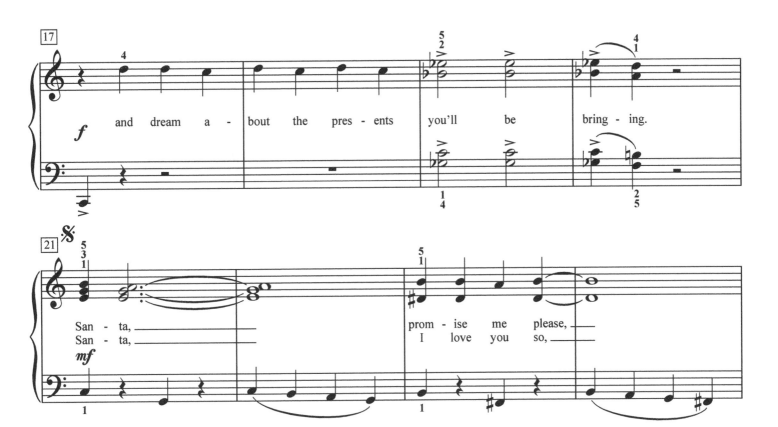

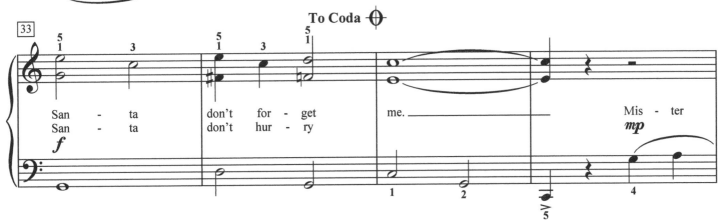

Santa, _____ dear old Saint Nick,

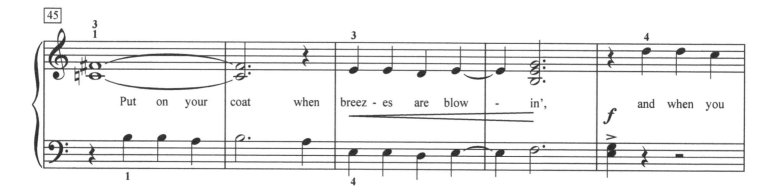

be aw - ful care - ful and please don't get sick. _____

Put on your coat when breez - es are blow - in', *f* and when you

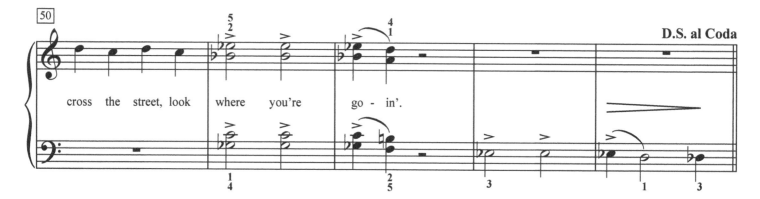

D.S. al Coda

cross the street, look where you're go - in'.

CODA

back. _____ *p* *ff*

Somewhere in My Memory

from the Twentieth Century Fox Motion Picture HOME ALONE

Words by Leslie Bricusse
Music by John Williams
Arranged by Mona Rejino

Gently and with simplicity (♩ = 76)

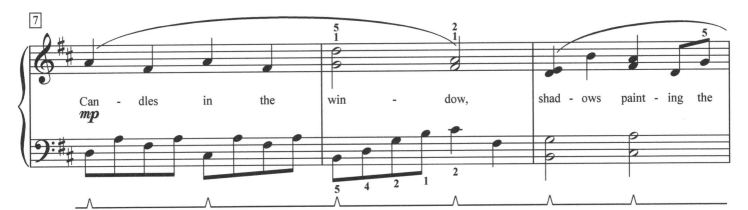

Can - dles in the win - dow, shad - ows paint - ing the

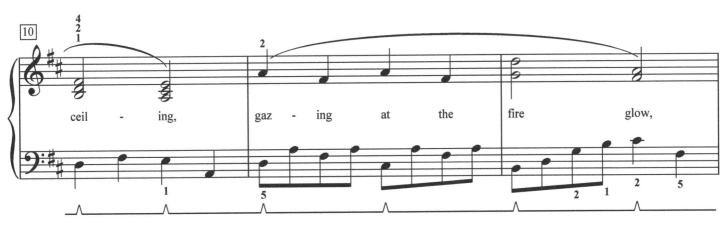

ceil - ing, gaz - ing at the fire glow,

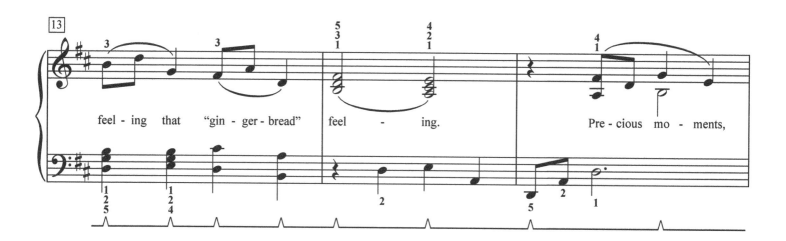

feel - ing that "gin - ger - bread" feel - ing. Pre - cious mo - ments,

spe - cial peo - ple, hap - py fac - es I can see.

simile

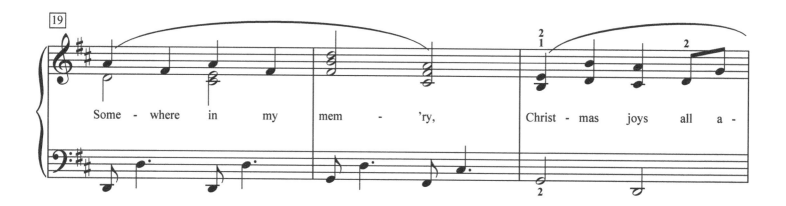

Some - where in my mem - 'ry, Christ - mas joys all a -

round me, liv - ing in my mem - 'ry.

All of the mu - sic, all of the mag - ic, all of the fam - 'ly

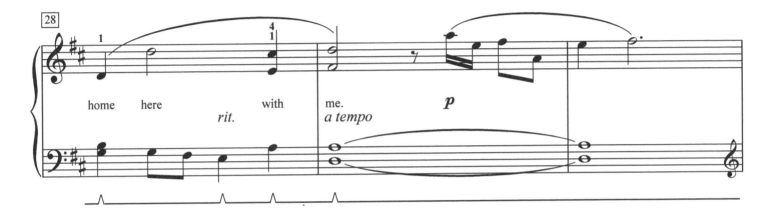

home here *rit.* with me. *a tempo* **p**

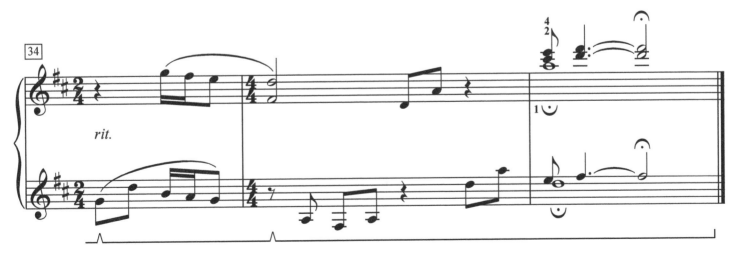

rit.

Skating

By Vince Guaraldi
Arranged by Phillip Keveren

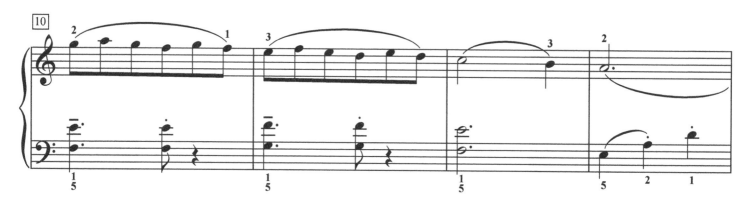

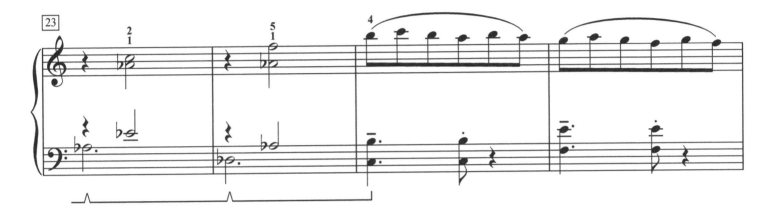

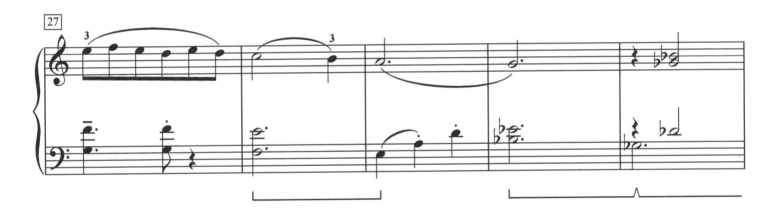

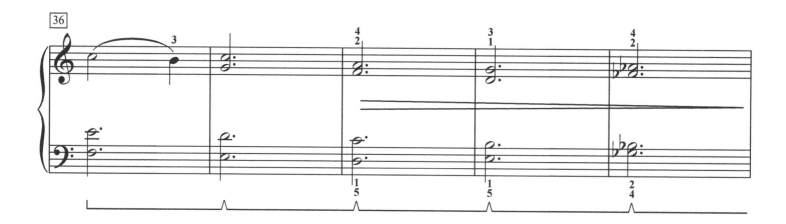

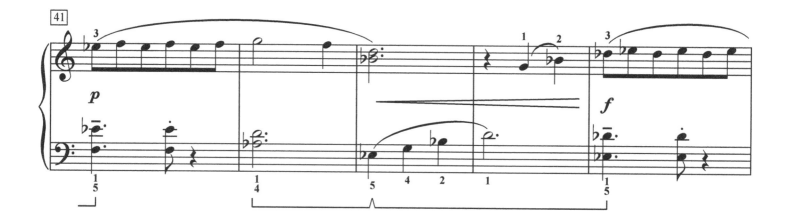

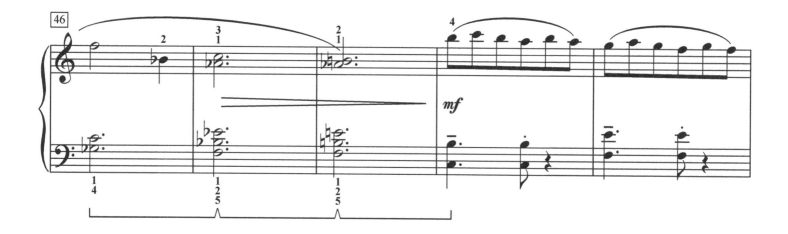

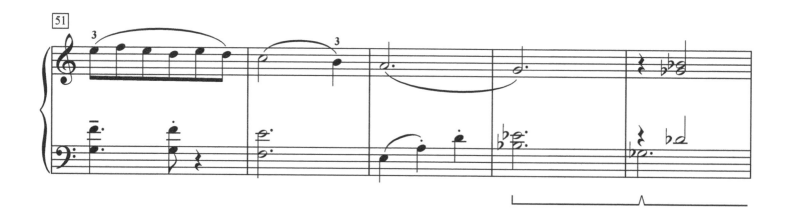

Tennessee Christmas

Words and Music by Amy Grant
and Gary Chapman

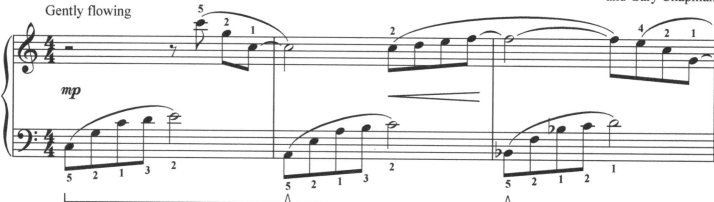

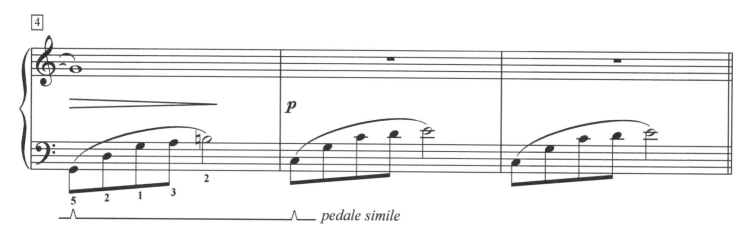

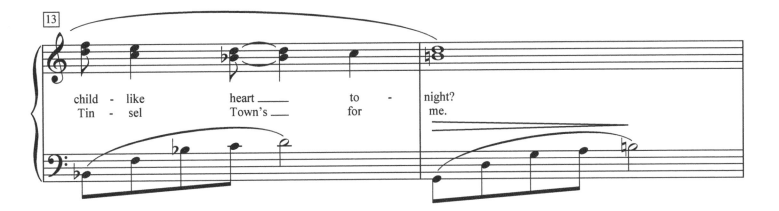

child - like heart ____ to - night?
Tin - sel Town's ____ for me.

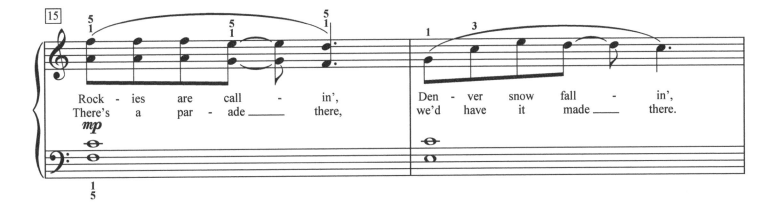

Rock - ies are call - in',
There's a par - ade ____ there,

Den - ver snow fall - in',
we'd have it made ____ there.

Some - bod - y said ____ it's
Bring home a tan ____ for

four ____ feet deep. ____ But
New ____ Year's Eve. ____

it does - n't mat - ter,
Sure sounds ex - cit - ing,

give me the laugh - ter,
aw - f'lly in - vit - ing,

Toyland
from BABES IN TOYLAND

Words by Glen MacDonough
Music by Victor Herbert

Tenderly

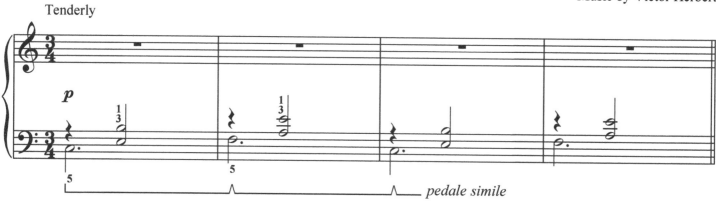

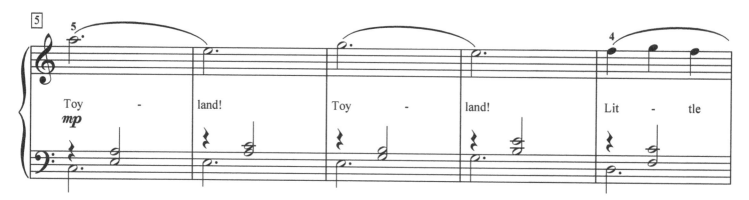

Toy - land! Toy - land! Lit - tle

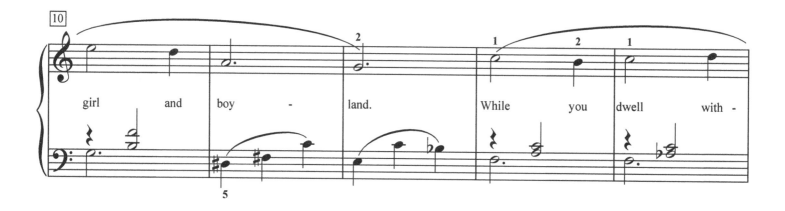

girl and boy - land. While you dwell with -

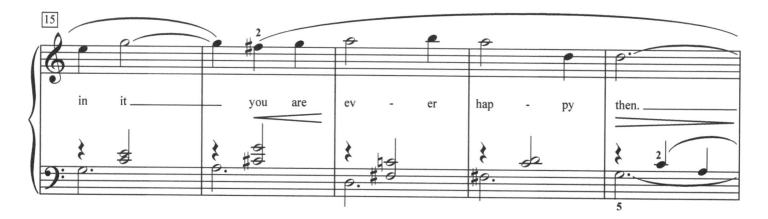

in it you are ev - er hap - py then.

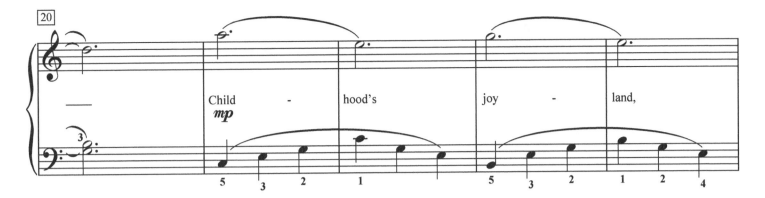

Child - hood's joy - land,

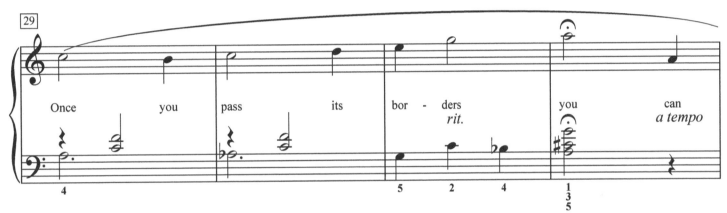

mys - tic mer - ry Toy - land!

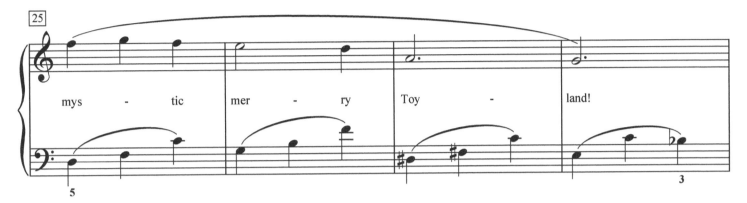

Once you pass its bor - ders you can

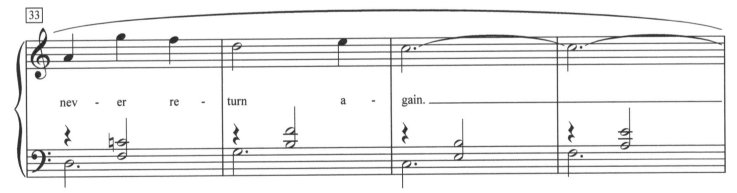

nev - er re - turn a - gain.

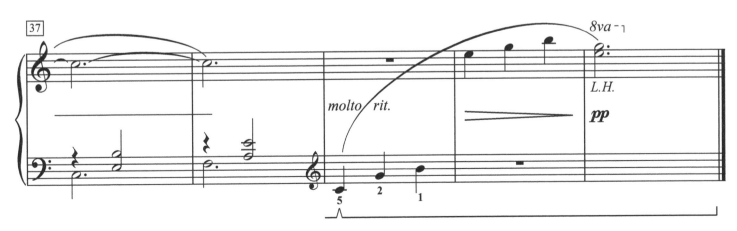

White Christmas
from the Motion Picture Irving Berlin's HOLIDAY INN

Words and Music by
Irving Berlin
Arranged by Phillip Keveren

Brightly, with sparkle (♩ = 160)

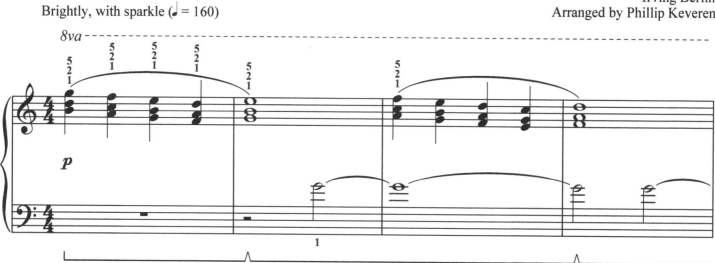

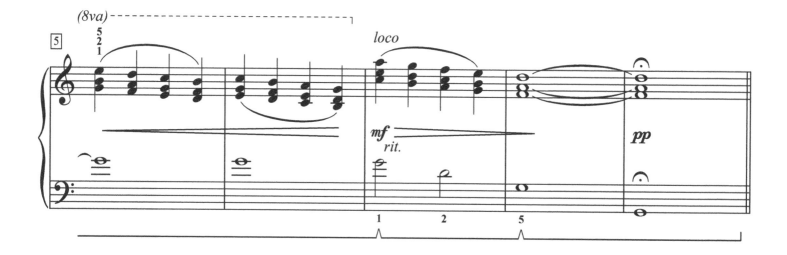

Slowly, with nostalgia (♩ = 108)

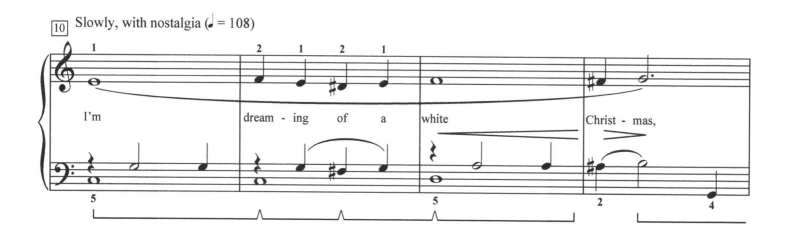

I'm dream - ing of a white Christ - mas,

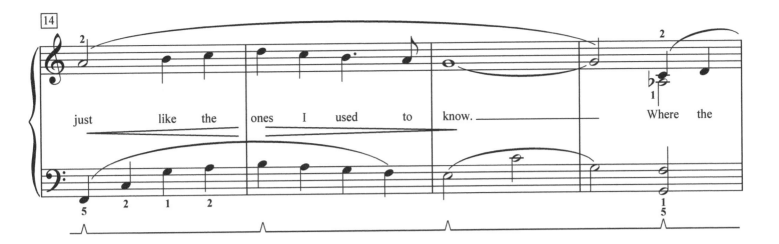

just   like   the   ones I used   to   know.   Where   the

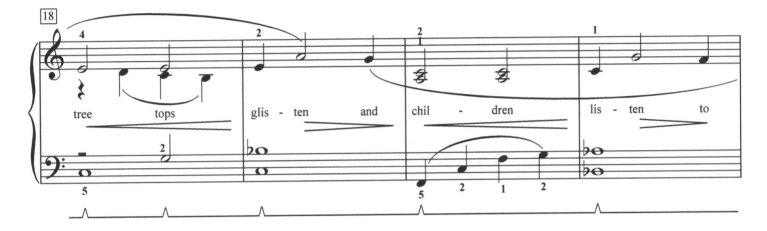

tree   tops   glis - ten and   chil - dren   lis - ten   to

hear   sleigh - bells in the   snow.

p   *mf*

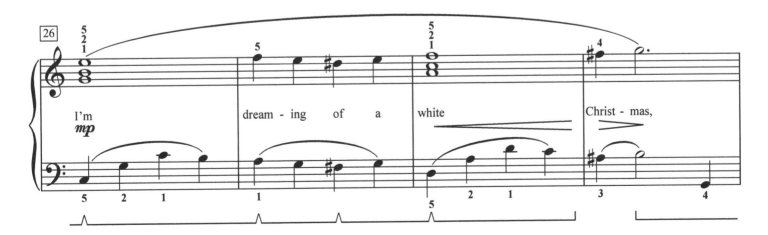

I'm   dream - ing of   a   white   Christ - mas,

mp

with ev - 'ry Christ - mas card I write: _____ "May your

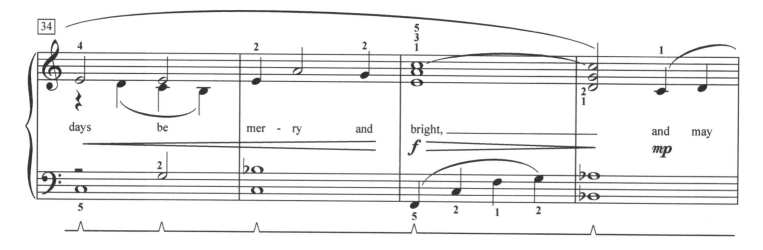

days be mer - ry and bright, _____ and may

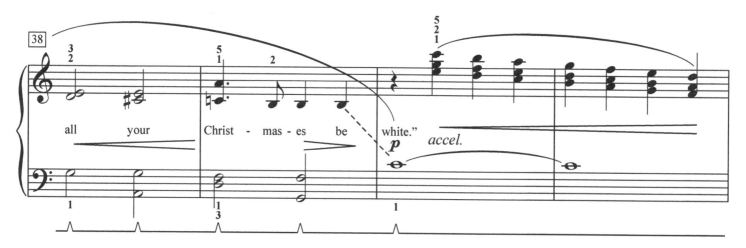

all your Christ - mas - es be white." accel.

rit. I'm dream - ing of a

mf a tempo

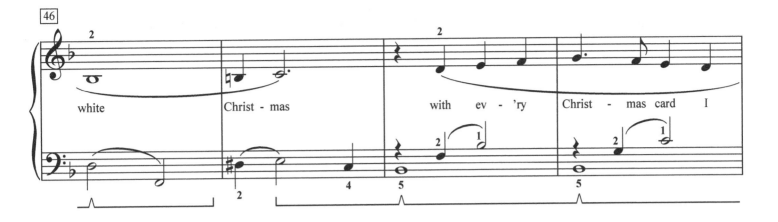

white   Christ - mas   with ev - 'ry   Christ - mas card I

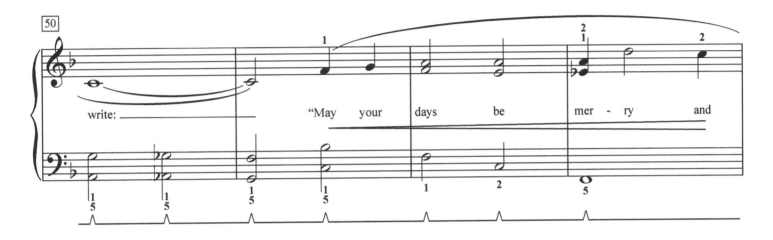

write: _____   "May   your   days   be   mer - ry   and

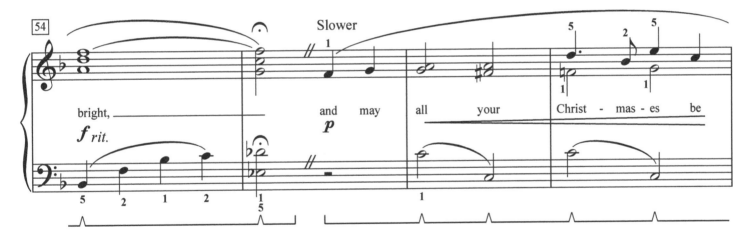

bright, _____   Slower and may all   your   Christ - mas - es be
f *rit.*   *p*

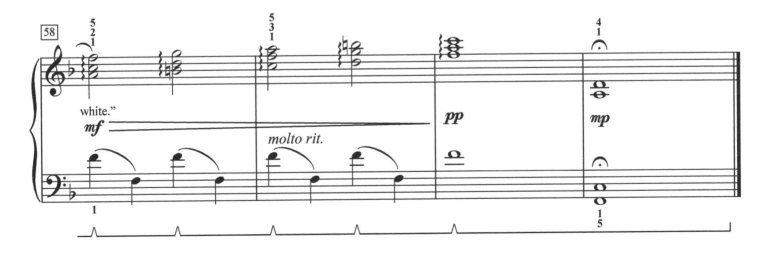

white."   *pp*   *mp*
mf _____   *molto rit.*

We Need a Little Christmas

from MAME

Music and Lyric by
Jerry Herman
Arranged by Carol Klose

Bright Polka tempo (♩ = 100)

Haul / climb out / down the hol / chim - ly, / ney, _____ put / turn up / on the

tree / bright be - / -est fore / string my / of spir - / lights it / I've falls / ev - a - / er gain; / seen.

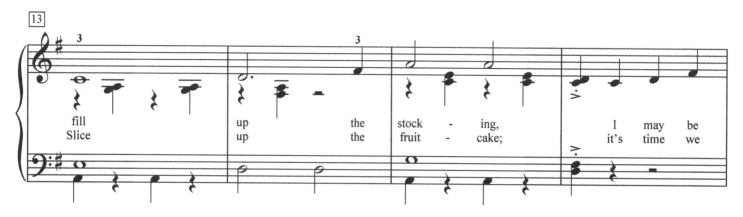

fill / Slice up / up the stock - / fruit ing, / cake; I / it's may / time be / we

rush - ing | things, but | deck the halls ____ a - gain
hung some | tin - sel | on that ev - er - green

now. ____
bough. ____
cresc.

For we
For I've
f

need a litt - tle | Christ - mas, | right this ver - y | min - ute,
grown a lit - tle | lean - er, | grown a lit - tle | cold - er,
need a lit - tle | mu - sic, | need a lit - tle | laugh - ter,

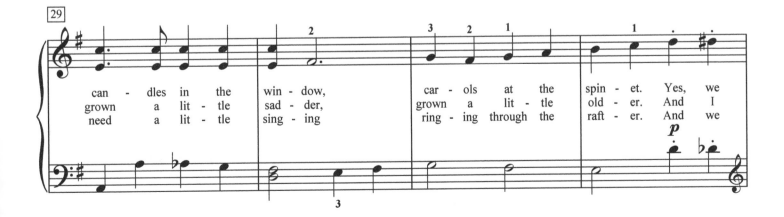

can - dles in the | win - dow, | car - ols at the | spin - et. Yes, we
grown a lit - tle | sad - der, | grown a lit - tle | old - er. And I
need a lit - tle | sing - ing | ring - ing through the | raft - er. And we
p

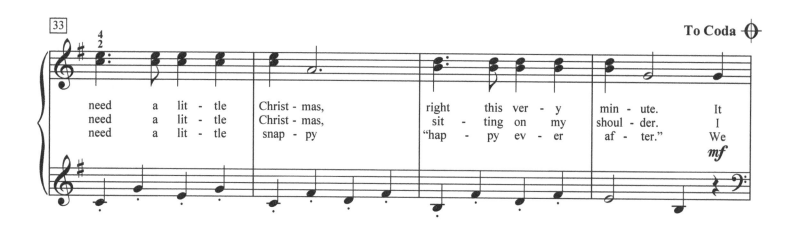

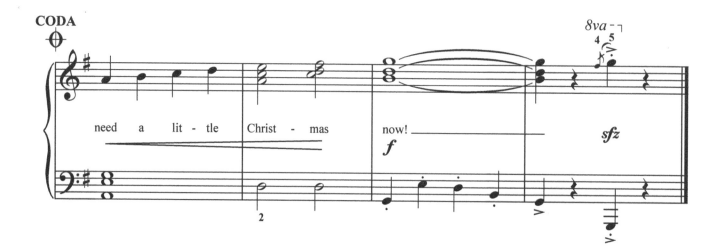